busy
LITTLE
KIDS

NEVA ELLIOTT

Busy Little Kids by Neva Elliott

Published by Jane Curry Publishing 2014

PO Box 780, Edgecliff, NSW 2027
AUSTRALIA
www.janecurrypublishing.com.au

National Library of Australia cataloguing-in-publication data:

Author: Neva Elliott
Title: Busy Little Kids
ISBN 978-192518-300-9

Photographs: Neva Elliott, Shelley Lawnikanis, Stephanie Tait, Shutterstock
Cover: Shelley Lawnikanis
Internal design by Working Type
Production: Jasmine Standfield
Printed by 1010 Printing International Limited in China

Disclaimer
Young children need to be supervised around water activities, activities that involve scissors, gluing or cutting and activities involving small objects.

To little dreamers everywhere; and two in particular
— Josie and Ryan. Remember, darkness only exists
so the stars can shine, my darlings.

"Logic will get you from A to B, imagination will take you everywhere".

Imagination is an intangible thing that sparkles with possibility. Studies have shown that children with active imaginations are happier, more alert and better able to cope with life's ups and downs, all things that most parents wish for their children.

As a mother of two young children I found myself relying on technology to keep my kids entertained and I knew I had to make a change. I wanted my kids to experience the same childhood I had. A time filled with wonder, exploring and creating, making mud pies, building cubby houses and threading daisy chains — all things that at the time, didn't seem particularly important, but looking back are the happiest memories from my childhood.

Technology has its place in our homes and lives today; however to learn about the world, children need to look, listen, touch, feel and taste things. Time away from technology allows a child's creativity to grow and gets their growing bodies moving. Exploring nature teaches children to respect and love the outdoors, a relationship that can last a lifetime. Outdoors as well as indoors can be magical with the right ideas and tools.

This book is for parents who, like me, are sometimes stuck for ideas. When little faces are peering up at you I hope this collection of activities can help. Each activity in the book can be adapted to suit the age of your child; younger children will need a parent's help, while older children can play solo or change the activity to suit their style of play. The importance of enjoying your own company cannot be underestimated; if a child can entertain themselves, they have a friend for life.

Whether they are little explorers, magicians or scientists, whether sitting quietly observing and daydreaming, or jumping around wildly singing and dancing, given the opportunity, children can discover magic in the simplest of things. Enjoy!

SUNNY DAY ☀ IDEAS

Colour Matching

Here is a creative way to use old paint swatches. Give your child a selection of colours and help them search around the house and garden to find things that match. This is a great way for them to learn about colours and shades.

Magic Flowers

Fill a glass or vase with water and stir in a few drops of food colouring.
Take a fresh white flower such as a carnation, snip the end off the stem and
place it in the water. Wave your hands, wait a few hours and abracadabra!
The flower will begin to change colour. Shhh, here's the secret; as the water
travels up the stem and into the petals, it carries the colour with it. Truly magical
for little ones. and it makes a great science experiment for older kids.

Sound Safari

Take a walk around your neighbourhood, local park or backyard and listen to all the sounds. Find a comfy place to sit. Close your eyes and be very still. What can you hear? The wind blowing, dogs barking? Perhaps birds chirping, bees buzzing, or leaves rustling? This is a lovely activity to teach children how wonderful silence can be.

Nature Collage

Go searching around your garden or local park and collect some leaves, flowers, twigs, seeds or shells. Then, using some glue and your imagination, transform them into a beautiful piece of art. Perhaps it will be a picture of a magical garden, a seascape or a castle.

Outdoor Movies

Make your own drive-in movies at home. Set up a laptop on the grass or patio and lay out some sleeping bags or blankets. Make some popcorn and pick out your child's favourite movie. Even if you have seen it a hundred times it's always more magical out under the stars. If you're feeling especially creative, a few fairy lights will make the atmosphere even more enchanting.

Dinosaur Dig

Put on your overalls and helmet because it's time to go digging. Hide a few toy dinosaurs around the yard, in the sandpit or at the beach, then grab a bucket and spade and start searching. Alternatively, chicken bones make great pretend dinosaur fossils so your children will feel like real life archaeologists.

Pet Rock

This one is so popular, *Time* Magazine named it one of the top 10 toy crazes of all time. Pet rocks originated back in the 1970s but they're still just as fun today! Simply find a rock, give it a name, draw on a face and 'voila', you have your very own pet. Better yet, it doesn't need walking or feeding. If you want to be really creative you can stick on eyes, felt ears and use glitter pens; your child's imagination is the limit.

Fruit Shapes

Fruit is much more fun when it is cut into little shapes. There's a cookie cutter for every shape you can imagine — try making a star, a heart or your child's favourite animal. A great idea for those fussy eaters. Try using watermelon, pineapple or rockmelon.

Ice Cube Painting

Add a few drops of different food colouring to water in an ice cube tray and freeze. A few hours later you'll have some 'water crayons' that are perfect for drawing on paper as they melt. You can even try freezing paddle pop sticks into the ice cubes to help with painting. A wonderful summertime activity.

Balloons

Never underestimate how much children love balloons. Next time you're stuck
for something to do, grab some balloons and have some fun! There are so many
games to play with balloons; try seeing who can keep the balloon in the air the
longest, or have a game of balloon tennis. You can make a racquet out
of a wooden spoon and paper plate.

Feed the Ducks

Gather up all your old bits of bread and venture out to your local lake or a nearby park. Children love interacting with animals and enjoy the simple task of throwing the bread. Try feeding the ducks and fish in the lake, or the birds in the park or your backyard.

Footpath Artwork

All you need is a few sticks of chalk and a footpath, sidewalk, patio or even a driveway. Making an artwork on something this big is much more fun than just the old blackboard. This is a great activity for hand-eye co-ordination and fine motor skills in younger children.

Get Up Close

Everything looks better when it's super-sized, so grab a magnifying glass and go searching around the garden. You'll be amazed how fascinating the bugs and flowers are when you're looking at them up close. Using the new discoveries your children have made, encourage them to draw their favourite thing from the garden in as much detail as possible.

Splat Painting

This one can get a little messy but children absolutely love it. You can use an outside wall or fence, or a blackboard covered in paper. Get a few old tennis balls, drop them in a bowl with a mixture of paint and water, and throw them at the wall. It creates some wonderful shapes and patterns. Your children will love their artwork and it will help their hand-eye co-ordination and motor skills.

Car Washing

Anything involving water is fun, especially on a warm sunny day. Grab a bucket of soapy water and a sponge, and get to work making those toy trucks and cars shine. The older children can even help wash the family car.

Lemonade Stand

Lemons, cold water, sugar and crushed ice is all you need to make the perfect lemonade. If you want to be extra creative you could add oranges and make orangeade. Once it tastes perfect, set up a lemonade stand or host a lemonade party for all your teddies.

Water Painting

Who needs paint when water is a great alternative? Gather together some paintbrushes and a pot of water. Then select your canvas; it could be coloured paper, newspapers, bricks, concrete, a fence, the patio or outside walls. Then all you have to do is dip your brush into the water and you're away! Painting in the sun will evaporate quickly, or try painting in the shade to make it last longer.

DON'T FORGET TO ...

 Pick wild flowers

 Make mud pies

 Walk barefoot in the grass

 Wish on a dandelion

Gardening

Gardening is great fun. Children love to watch the progress of their plants as they bloom and grow in front of their eyes. There are lots of plants young children can grow without too much trouble, from small trees to herbs and vegetables. If you don't have a garden try a window box or small pots, and if you grow herbs like basil and parsley, you can eat them once they've grown.

Slip & Slide

Hose + tarpaulin + soap = heaven for children.

Make A Bird Feeder

Here's a great way to attract the local birds to your garden. Cut a hole through the centre of an old juice or milk carton that is large enough for birds to fit inside. Then make two small holes on either side of the carton below the opening so that you can push a branch through; this makes a little perch for the birds. Scatter some birdseed on the floor of the bottle, attach some string around the top and hang it from a tree in your garden. Then it's time to sit back and watch all your new visitors arrive!

Fly A Kite

Don't let a windy day go by without flying a kite. This is fun for all ages and great exercise too. Let one fly in your backyard or down by the beach for guaranteed smiles.

Tie-Dying

This is a flashback to the 70's that the kids will love. Tie-dying is a great way to invigorate old clothes and is lots of fun. Simply grab a piece of clothing, roll it, tie it with rubber bands or twist it, then leave it to soak in fabric dye. Experiment with a range of different designs, your children will be amazed at their creation.

Star Gazing At Dusk

Pick a clear night where the stars are at their brightest and lie down on a blanket outside. Point out the different constellations to older children and show the smaller children some interesting shapes and patterns. This can be a magical time to spend with your child, as you watch the wonder and amazement on their face. If you're lucky you might even see a shooting star.

Water Play

Fill up a large bucket or tub with water and give your child some scoops, bowls, cups and toys. It's great to have a variety of things that float and sink. You can add a few drops of food colouring for some extra fun. Remember to supervise young children closely.

Ant Detective

Simple but so much fun! Let your child pick out an ant in the garden to follow around. They'll be fascinated with where it goes and what it does. See what happens when you give it a crumb or encourage it to walk along a leaf.

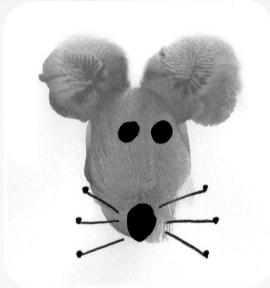

Thumbprint Painting

Using a stamp pad or some paint, let your child press their fingers or thumb into the colours and then onto a piece of paper. Create characters by adding features with a pencil, pen, or marker. Make a mouse, a fairy or a space ship — the possibilities are endless.

Cloud Shapes

Pick a day when there are plenty of fluffy clouds around and find a comfy place
to lie with your child. Point out all the shapes you see and watch how they
move and change with the wind. Can you spot a monkey, a giant crocodile,
or a fire-breathing dragon?

Treasure Hunt

You can't go past a treasure hunt when you're looking for a fun activity for kids.
Hide a few things in the garden or house and then go and search with your
child. You can help the younger children by telling them what they are looking
for. Give older children a few hints; say 'warmer' or 'colder' or even draw
a treasure map. This is great for your child's cognitive development
— helping them to learn and solve problems.

Balance Beam

Teetering along something thin is always a fun challenge for children.
Your balance beam doesn't have to be up high, you can make a tight rope with
some string along the ground. Let your child can use their imagination;
maybe they're on the roof of a tall building or creeping along the edge
of a mountain? This activity works well indoors or out and is great for
developing coordination and, (you guessed it) balance.

Paper Planes

This one is great for children of all ages. Let the older kids create their own planes and you can help the little ones fold theirs. Don't forget to decorate them with crayons, paint and design a logo. Launch them from a window or out in the garden and see which one goes the fastest and flies the furthest.

Hopscotch

An old favourite. Grab a piece of chalk and a few pebbles and you're set.
Draw out your hopscotch map and away you go! This classic game is great
for children's balance and co-ordination and, best of all, it's lots of fun.

Have A Tea Party

Tea parties aren't just for girls…you can tell the boys it's a lunch party.
Perfect for a sunny afternoon; set up your rug in the garden with some teapots,
cups and sandwiches. Invite some friends and ask them to bring their
favourite bear and make it a teddy bears' picnic.

Exercise

Children love doing what you're doing and exercise is no exception.
Try some simple yoga or Pilates on a mat, show your child the different positions
and see if they can copy you. Great exercise and lots of fun for you both.

Sunshine Reading

Get your child to choose a few of their favourite books and head outside
with a rug. Set yourselves up under a tree or umbrella in your backyard
or local park and let story time begin. This will give them an entirely
different experience to the usual bedtime story.

Hide & Seek

This classic children's game is great played indoors or out.
For younger children you can try hiding a toy and finding it together.

Water Balloons

This activity is always a big hit with children and is a great idea for a summer's day. Young children will have fun simply squishing the balloon between their hands, while the older children will love throwing, catching and dropping the balloons around the yard.

DON'T FORGET TO ...

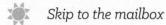 *Skip to the mailbox*

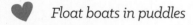 *Float boats in puddles*

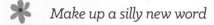 *Make up a silly new word*

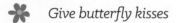 *Give butterfly kisses*

Fly Swatter Painting

Making art and along with it, a big mess, is a rite of passage for children. Grab a fly swatter, paper and some coloured paints. Put a dollop of paint on the paper and let the art making begin! Children will get a thrill out of swatting with the fly swatter and they'll be enthralled with the patterns it makes when it hits the paper. Probably best to keep this one outside.

Make Your Own Rainbow

On a sunny day head out to the garden. Standing with the sun behind you, turn on the hose and spray it in a curved shape. Look at the rainbow that appears. The little ones love this; they can run under it, jump through it and even search for the pot of gold at the end!

Sprinkler Fun

Running through the sprinkler is one of the greatest joys of childhood.
Kids love anything involving water, and this is a great way to cool down
on a warm day and instantly puts children in a good mood.

Grow Your Own Beanstalk

Watching a plant grow is perhaps the most simple and wondrous thing. All you need is a clear glass or plastic cup, some cotton balls and a bean — butter beans, broad beans and lima beans all work, and can be found in the dry foods section of your supermarket. Place a few beans on the sides of the cup and cover with cotton balls. Water until damp (but not wet) and place on the windowsill. Within 4-5 days the bean will begin to grow! Your children will love watching it emerge from the cotton and grow into a stalk. Magic!

Toy Bath Time

Your toys get dirty too so be sure to give them a nice bubble bath. Gather up your teddies, dolls or animals and scrub them till they're squeaky clean. Children love this activity, for once they are the ones giving the bath rather than receiving it.

Cotton Bud Painting

Using cotton buds as paint brushes is a rather dainty art exercise for your child that will help develop their artistic ability, as well as their fine motor skills. This one is all about the little details which children love; draw a lady bug with spots or a Dalmatian puppy. You could also try making dot art.

Hill Rolling

Children have enjoyed this simple pastime for generations. All you need is a nice grassy hill with a slight incline, and get rolling. If you're near the beach you could also slide down the dunes on a boogie board. Either way it's like a fantastic slippery dip and roller coaster rolled into one! A great way to get in touch with your inner child.

Daisy Chains

As beautiful as they are simple. Ignite your inner hippie and create your own flower chain. Simply pierce a little hole in the bottom of each stem with your thumbnail and thread the next stem through. You can make bracelets or necklaces; your children will love the jewellery they've created.

Sensory Garden

Using some simple items like rice, pasta and herbs from the garden you can
create your own miniature garden landscape. You could make a forest using
small jungle figures with big boulders and tall trees, or maybe a seaside
with some blue colouring and toy fish. Children will love having
their own little scene to play with.

I Spy

An old favourite that is too often forgotten. I Spy is great at home or on
a long car ride. For the little ones try giving bigger clues like
"I spy with my little eye something big and warm in the sky."

Outdoor Cubby

Children love to hide and cubby houses are a childhood rite of passage. Cubbies can be as elaborate or as simple as you like. Try using a sheet draped over some chairs or a tree branch, or an old shower curtain threaded through a hula hoop.

Backyard Cooking

Using sand, water, shells, straw and herbs from the garden, set up your own little outdoor kitchen. Children love playing with all the different textures, and you can use anything you have available. Add a few cups, spoons and a saucepan and you can look forward to some tasty mud pie or leaf soup for dinner. Delish!

Ball Pit

You don't have to go to a playground to play in a ball pit; you can make your own at home. Fill up a small wading pool, playpen or cot with colourful plastic balls. Children love the feeling of rolling and falling through the balls and they make a great place to hide. You can easily pick up large bags of balls at your local dollar store or online.

Four Leaf Clover

Enjoy the sunshine while you hunt for the elusive four-leaf clover. Who knows, perhaps you'll find a little leprechaun hiding in the tiny heart-shaped leaves? Most parks or grassy areas have clovers growing in amongst the grass.

Magical Fairy Garden

Guess what? A family of fairies have moved into the garden! Set up a special garden bed or potted plant with flowers and pebbles so they can really call it home. Make sure you give them special fairy names and see if you can spot them when they appear. This is a wonderful imaginative play activity that your child can return to each day.

Night Time Torch Adventure

Take a walk as night falls and explore your environment. You can go as far as you like, maybe to the end of the street or just stick to your backyard or patio. The world outside changes at dusk, and wonderful things happen as darkness sets in. Use a torch and see what you can find. Is there anything hiding in the trees, are the geckos venturing out, and what about moths and fireflies?

Construction Watching

Next time you go past a building site, slow down and watch for a little while.
Often children have only seen these huge machines on television or in books,
and are fascinated to watch them in real-life action. Listen to the engines and
the reversing beep, watch them scoop and dig. What will they create?

Bear Hunt

Pick out a few of your child's favourite soft toys and hide them around the yard or house. Teddies make the perfect hide and seek friends. You can make it easier or harder depending on the age of your child.

Make A Magic Potion

Encourage your little magician or scientist to make their own magic potion.
You can use anything you have on hand like milk, water, food dye, flowers, grass
or washing up liquid. Give them a few containers, spoons, cups and perhaps a
funnel. Then they are all set to mix, pour, swish and tip to their heart's content.
What weird and wonderful potions will their imaginations create?

DON'T FORGET TO ...

 Skim stones

 Give piggy back rides to bed

 Climb a tree

 Listen to a sea shell

Painting With Flowers

Before you throw away those flowers on your dining table you can use them for this fun art activity. Dip the petals in some paint and press them onto paper to create beautiful shapes. This is a wonderful way to enjoy nature and art at the same time. You could also use wild flowers picked from your garden and even try leaves and grass as well.

Watch The Sun Set

Dusk can be a tricky time of day for little ones as they can get tired and grizzly,
so why not get out of the house and pack up a picnic dinner? Head out to
the yard or your local park and watch the sky change colour as the sun sets.
Together you can search for the first evening star to appear in the night sky.

Share The Chores

Children love to be involved and feel like they're helping, so what may seem tedious for you can be a lot of fun for them. Try emptying the dishwasher or hanging and folding washing together. As children get older they will be more inclined to help with chores as they enjoy the feeling of responsibility.

Tennis Racket Bubbles

Sometimes the best activities happen by accident! Who would have thought a bucket of detergent with glycerol, or bubble solution and a plastic racket could create so much fun? Children both young and old are mesmerised by bubbles. Watch them as they float through the air, shining with different colours. Then chase the bubbles to see how the wind blows them along until they pop! The tennis racket creates lots of large bubbles at once. Forget just blowing bubbles, this is way more fun.

Make Your Own Perfume

Why not make your very own perfume using some flowers from the garden?
Select a few of your favourite blooms, press gently to extract the scent,
and pop in a pretty jar or bottle with some water. Voila, you've got your
very own personalised scent.

Magic Wands

Did you know that you can find the perfect magic wand in your garden? Search the yard together to find one or surprise your child with one — perhaps a fairy or a wizard left one in the yard for them? Once you find the perfect stick you can make some magic. Maybe you can make flowers grow or get the garden ants to walk in a straight line? Hours of enjoyment, so easy and completely free.

RAINY DAY ☂ IDEAS

Build A Fort

Great for hiding, playing or reading. All you need are some sheets and a few chairs. Scatter some cushions inside and hang up some fairy lights to make it even more magical. Encourage your child's imagination as they create their own little world inside. They could play house, build a secret castle, or even have a picnic in the cubby for lunch.

Activity Lucky Dip

Sit down with your little ones and help them write a list of all their favourite things to do. Place all the ideas into a special jar and next time they are bored have a lucky dip to choose an activity.

Button Art

Kids love arts and crafts and this is a great activity to create something they can
keep, and a way to use up all your odd buttons. On a piece of cardboard, help
your child draw an outline of their favourite picture; birds, trains and hot air
balloons always look great. Use a collection of buttons to 'colour in' your picture.
Bags of buttons are available at craft stores and op-shops.

Pretend Holiday

Today we're off to Fiji, Disneyland, London or the snow! Make a 'passport' with your child's name and a little sketch of them. You could even make some aeroplane tickets. Then it's time to pack a bag and off you go! At the 'airport' you need to check in and have your bags x-rayed (use an empty box with the ends open, or slide the bags along the lounge) then it's off to the boarding gate. Make some snacks for the inflight meal, perhaps watch a movie, then snap some pictures when you arrive. Bon voyage!

Puddle Jumping

Perhaps the simplest child's activity but also the most fun. If there's
been rain around venture outside because there's sure to be one thing...
Puddles! Yes they will get wet and muddy, but the pure joy on their little faces is
absolutely worth it. A perfect afternoon activity so children can get into a nice
warm bath afterwards.

Indoor Beach

When it's raining outside why not bring the beach to you? Help your child
to draw some sunny pictures and stick them up around the lounge room.
Grab your beach umbrella, some towels, hats, snacks and books.
An easy way to brighten up a gloomy day.

Teddy Bear Party

Hang up some colourful bunting, put on your party hats and invite all your favourite teddy bears because it's time to have a party. Play your favourite music, sing songs, and, if you have time, wrap up some pretend presents.

Shadow Animals

Simply find a bare wall and use a torch or lamp that casts a shadow.
See how many animals you can create — try making a butterfly,
a bird or a rabbit.

Cardboard Creative

No matter how great the present is, it's often the box it came in that intrigues little children the most. A simple cardboard box provides endless possibilities. Watch it become a boat, a car, a house or even a spaceship. All you need is a few colouring pens and your child's wonderful imagination. Your local appliance store often has spare large boxes that are great for this activity.

Indoor Bowling

Create your own bowling alley at home using recycled plastic bottles. Set up the
'pins' in your hallway or lounge room and use a soft ball to roll down the lane.
This is a great activity for hand-eye co-ordination and is always lots of fun.
Strike!

Magic Milk

This is a simple science experiment that is fun to do and a great way to help your children learn about how substances interact. Pour some milk into a bowl and add a few drops of different food colouring, as well as a drop of dishwashing liquid. Now watch the colours swirl around in wonderful patterns. Magic!

Dress Ups

Dress up play is an important part of a child's development. Gather together some old shirts, purses, sunglasses and hats and keep them in a special chest or box. Then let your children rummage through and choose a special outfit.
I think I hear a princess stuck in a castle?

Straw Puppets

Time to get the pens and pencils out and draw some characters. Animals, fairies or superheroes all make great straw puppets. Cut the characters out of paper and stick each character onto a drinking straw. These are easy to hold and children can use them to act out a story like Goldilocks and the Three Bears, or an underwater world with dancing dolphins and talking shells.

DON'T FORGET TO ...

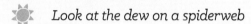 *Look at the dew on a spiderweb*

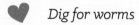 *Dig for worms*

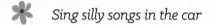 *Sing silly songs in the car*

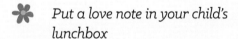 *Put a love note in your child's lunchbox*

Indoor Basketball

You don't always need a basketball and a goal to shoot hoops. Simply scrunch up some pieces of paper and set up a bucket or box, then take it in turns with your child to score 'goals'. This is great fun for toddlers and a wonderful activity for developing hand-eye coordination. It's also an excellent way to get some use out of all those old newspapers.

Would You Rather...?

A perfect game for beating boredom, especially on long car rides. Think up some creative questions to ask your kids like 'would you rather have breakfast for dinner, or dinner for breakfast?' or 'would you rather be a dog or a cat or a mouse?' or 'would you rather fly to the moon or swim to the bottom of the sea?' Be sure to ask 'why?' because the answers are the best part.

Visit The Library

Why not encourage your children to immerse themselves in a world
of literary adventure by taking a trip to the library? Most local libraries have
activity groups for children of all ages such as rhyming and singing for younger
children, and story-time and reading groups for the older kids.
There's something for everyone at the library!

Musical Jars

This game helps your child learn about sounds and musical notes.
Collect some jars and fill them with varying amounts of water so you have lots
of different levels. Add some food colouring to each jar so the levels are obvious
to younger children. Give your child a spoon and let them gently tap each glass,
noting the different sounds they make. They can arrange the glasses
from the lowest to highest water level and make up a song.

Homemade Jewellery

This is an easy craft activity for children and assists with the development of fine motor skills. Place some uncooked pasta and a few drops of food colouring into a ziplock bag, shake and allow to dry. Then thread the pasta onto a string (you can use a match at one end to make the threading easier) to create necklaces and bracelets.

Make A Crown

This is a perfect autumn activity. Use some fallen leaves from the trees
in your garden or local park to make a crown. Measure out a strip of cardboard
to fit your child's head, then simply stick on your leaves with glue.
You could also add some tin foil to make a shiny crown.

Rice And Beans Tub

Children love anything that involves tipping, scooping and pouring.
Uncooked rice and beans are perfect for this. All you need is a tub, some scoops,
cups, rice and beans. Then let them scoop and pour to their hearts' content.
Be sure to supervise young children closely. Easy to sweep or vacuum up once
they are finished, and store in a ziplock bag for next time.

Teddy Bear Hospital

Oh dear, the teddies aren't feeling so well, we had better take them to the doctor.
Use an old shirt for a doctor's coat, grab some bandages, pillows and blankets
and start bringing in your teddy patients. A dolls stroller or a washing basket
could be the ambulance. Don't forget a notepad and pen for writing prescriptions
and a flashlight for checking sore throats and ears.

Act Out A Book

Ignite your child's creative side by helping them act out their favourite book. Once you've chosen the book, select an outfit and some props. This activity is great for the imagination, as well as speech and language development. You could even make up a new story line for extra laughs.

DON'T FORGET TO ...

Smile when your child walks in the room

Tell them a story from your childhood

Put a flower in your hair

Take a train ride — for the journey not the destination

Make Your Own Puzzle

Using a picture from a magazine, or one of your children's drawings —
stick it onto some cardboard and then cut it into several pieces of various sizes.
You can make it easier or harder depending on the shapes and sizes.
Then let them piece it back together. This is a great activity that helps to
develop problem-solving skills.

Put On A Puppet Show

Create a stage using old boxes or cushions with a towel or sheets as the curtain. Your children's favourite dolls and teddies can be the characters, or you could even make some sock puppets. Great for the imagination and hand-eye co-ordination.

Story Squares

Cut out some coloured pieces of cardboard and draw a picture on each one. Then shuffle the cards and pull them out one by one. Try to create a story with each of the cards you choose. The story will change each time as you select the cards in a different order, and the more cards you make, the more story lines you will have. Older children can tell their own stories, and younger ones will love playing with the colourful pictures.

Paper Chains

Paper chains are a great way to use up junk mail or old paper and they make lovely decorations too. Simply cut your paper into thin strips and tape or glue them into circles, then loop the circles through each other to create a chain.

Flower Pressing

This craft activity is perfect for children and also makes a lovely gift as it can be easily framed. Once you have chosen your flowers, simply put them between two sheets of paper and weigh them down with a heavy book for around three days. Pansies, freesias and roses are great for pressing, as well as herbs like lavender and rosemary.

Egg Faces

So simple and so much fun. A little face makes even the simplest of things more endearing. Use a permanent marker to draw faces on your eggs. This will not only amuse the kids now, but they'll get an extra kick out of it next time you whip up bacon and eggs for breakfast!

Ziplock Painting

Painting without the mess! Put a few blobs of different coloured paint into a ziplock bag then place it on a white piece of paper and sticky tape it to a flat surface. Children can use their fingers to push down on the bag and create shapes and colours. You can use the same paint over and over, making handprints and playing noughts and crosses.

Potato Press

Cut a potato in half and use a knife, or cookie cutter to carve out a pattern
like a star, triangle, circle or heart. Then use your potato as a stamp by dipping
it into a tray of paint and pressing it onto paper. Children will love creating
an artwork using their own handmade stamp. So easy!

Telephone Cans

All you need is two plastic cups or tin cans, and about 5 metres of string.
Pierce a hole in the bottom of each cup, feed the string through and tie a large
knot. Hold the can to your ear and make sure the string is pulled tight.
Now you can chat to your heart's content, or whisper back and forth.
Your children will think their new telephone is magic.

Photo Booth Fun

There's something so lovely about an old fashioned photo booth. Most shopping centres and activity centres have them so next time you're walking past one take the time to jump in with your children and pull your silliest faces. The photo strips are wonderful mementos and also make great gifts for family and friends.

What Would You Do

This is a brilliant game for encouraging your child's imagination. Ask your child questions like 'what would you do if a penguin in long socks asked you to lunch?' or 'what would you do if your bed was made of chocolate?' or 'what would you do if a caterpillar was wearing your pyjamas?" You are going to love their naturally creative answers.

Bubble Wrap Dancing

Firmly tape a piece of bubble wrap to a hard floor and start dancing! Children of all ages absolutely love this activity as it involves jumping and making noise. The little ones can crawl around and the older kids can dance and roll.

DON'T FORGET TO ...

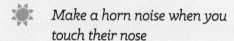 Make a horn noise when you touch their nose

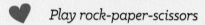 Play rock-paper-scissors

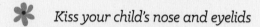 Kiss your child's nose and eyelids

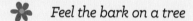 Feel the bark on a tree

Egg Carton Caterpillar

Get an old egg carton and cut it in half, separating the bottom egg cups from the lid. At one end draw on some eyes, then pierce two holes on top to thread through a pipe cleaner for antennae. Now you have your very own pet caterpillar. It's cute, and children get a great sense of accomplishment from playing with something they have made themselves.

Play Shop

Playing shop is a great game for children's imaginations. Such a simple and enjoyable activity can help develop your child's social skills, while teaching them about money and numbers. You could use some old shopping bags and tinned food from the pantry. They will be sharing, learning and communicating while playing in their pretend shop.

Little Wooly Lambs

Even very young children will enjoy this craft activity as they feel the texture of the cotton balls and have fun sticking with glue. Draw the outline of a sheep on some paper or cut one out of cardboard. Then stick on plenty of cotton wool so they are nice and fleecy and draw on a little face — so easy.

Pasta Art

Let your children create their own masterpiece using things from the pantry.
All you need is a few different types of pasta and some glue. Try macaroni, penne
and pasta shells. You could make a field of flowers, a space scene or a dinosaur.

Ice Cream Store

Using some old ice-cream containers and play dough you can set up your very own ice cream store. Try white for vanilla, pink for strawberry and brown for chocolate, or make up your own weird and wonderful ice cream flavours. Make a sign for your stand, then all you need are some scoops and bowls. Cotton balls also make great pretend ice cream.

Pipe Cleaner Fish

Who says you have to be outside to go fishing!? Twist some pipe cleaners into fish shapes and put them in a bucket. Then make a fishing hook out of another pipe cleaner and use this as your rod. For a longer fishing rod you could also attach some string to the end of your hook and tie it onto a ruler. See how many fish you can hook out of the bucket.

Indoor Golf

Have a game of indoor golf with a few household items. Turn an old ice cream container on its side; this is your hole, now gather up some golf balls and a putter. You can even put some obstacles in the way if you want to make it tricky. This is a fun activity for all ages and will help develop your child's hand-eye coordination.

Musical Chairs

There's a reason children have been playing musical chairs for generations;
it's easy, it's free and it's fun. If you only have one child then use some stuffed
animals to play with them (you can make them 'run' to a chair). Musical statues
is another variation that is great for one player; dance around and once the
music stops, they must freeze.

DON'T FORGET TO ...

 Leave bread and honey out for the ants

 Walk hand in hand

 Roll in piles of leaves

 Dance in the rain

Make Your Own Movie

Children love looking at themselves in photographs and moving pictures so why not get out your video camera or phone and make a little movie together? They could be singing, dancing, playing or painting. The awe on children's faces as they watch themselves is wonderful; they love being the star of the show.

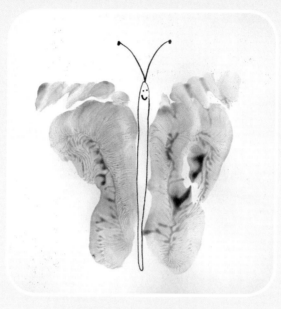

Butterfly Feet

While your child is sitting down, paint the soles of their feet with coloured paint (they'll love the tickly feeling), then press each foot down gently on some paper. Put the right foot on the left side and vice versa to create a butterfly shape. Then draw or paint a butterfly's body in the middle and voila, together you have created a beautiful piece of art.

Homemade Play Dough

Play dough is so simple to make at home. Simply mix 2 cups of flour, 1 cup of water, 1 cup of salt, a tablespoon of cooking oil and a few drops of food colouring. Your children will love helping out — squishing, rolling and making shapes. Store in a ziplock bag and if you're feeling really creative you can add some glitter for extra sparkle.

Cook Something

Sharing the kitchen with your child can inspire their interest in cooking.
It is also a fun way to encourage healthy eating habits. Try making a fruit
smoothie, a healthy pizza or some mashed potato. When cooking, children will
learn new words (like mix or peel) and develop an appreciation for doing things
step by step. They might also become more patient as they realise it was
worth waiting for those delicious muffins to cook.

Finger Puppets

Cut the fingers off an old rubber glove and draw a face on each one with a permanent marker. You'll now have your very own finger puppets and better yet, they're waterproof so are perfect for bath time playing.

Indoor Picnic

During those long rainy days when you can't venture outside why not set up an indoor picnic? Let your child help you pack the picnic basket, then lay out a blanket and some plates. After lunch, lie back on your blanket and imagine all the things you would see if you were outside. Are you at the beach, or by a lake? Are there birds flying by or dogs playing?

Ocean In A Bottle

A little twist on the classic message in a bottle. Create a sensory experience for your child in the form of an ocean bottle. Fill a plastic water bottle with some sand, shells, glitter, water, a few buttons and some plastic sea creatures. Then seal tightly and shake it up. Watching the different textures mix and float around has a calming effect on children, and they will love having their own little mini beach.

Dance Party

This one's simple. Just put on some music and dance! The conga line, the chicken dance, the limbo or the moon walk; dancing helps improve children's self-confidence, coordination and, of course, it's great exercise.

Gumboot Painting

Gumboots aren't just for splashing in muddy puddles, you can also use them for painting. Lay out some old pieces of cardboard or large pieces of paper and fill a plastic tray with different coloured paints. Pop on your gumboots, jump in the paint and let loose on your canvas. You can create footprint trails or wild patterns. This is a great activity to develop gross motor skills in young children.

DON'T FORGET TO ...

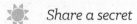 *Share a secret*

Draw pictures in the steam on the bathroom mirror

Make a cosy reading nook

Sprinkle pretend fairy dust on their pillows to help them sleep

Homemade Rain Gauge

Wouldn't you love to know how much rain is falling in a storm outside? Well you can with your own rain gauge. This is a simple experiment for children of all ages. Cut the top quarter off an old soft drink bottle, then place upside down inside the bottle to create a funnel, using sticky tape to secure. Next, mark the side of the bottle so you can measure how much rain has fallen. After each storm check on the rainfall and record your findings: was it a big thunder cloud or just a sprinkle?

Mandarin Snail

This simple, cute idea is perfect for snack time. Peel a mandarin and save
the skin; try and get it peeled in one long snake. Then using scissors carefully cut
out the shape of the snail's body and draw on a face. Now he needs a shell,
so place the mandarin on top. Finish it off by curving the body around.

Visit A Museum Or Art Gallery

A day at the museum or art gallery is a great way to see and learn about many new and exciting things, especially when the weather outside is gloomy. Marvel at the dinosaurs, sculptures and fossils. Admire the magnificent artworks and play a guessing game with the abstract paintings. Be sure to read the descriptions to your child. Check out dates with your local centres for special children's exhibitions.

Paint With Matchbox Cars

What little one doesn't love toy cars? Well, you can make them even better with the addition of some paint. Grab some paper and your favourite colours and use your cars as a brush. Drive them round the paper to create lines and swirls, then just throw them in some soapy water to clean when you're done.

Obstacle Course

Ready, set, go! Obstacle courses don't have to be outside; there are plenty of things you can use indoors. Roll along the lounge, crawl under the coffee table, hop to the door and jump over pillows, then repeat. Create the first course for your child and then let them use their imagination to build their own. You can make it as easy or hard as you like to suit the age of your child.

Float Or Sink

Will it float or will it sink? Children love this activity because it's like a tactile guessing game. Fill a bucket or large bowl with water and select a few objects from around the house; you could try an apple, a spoon, a washing peg or a key. Put them in the water one at a time. Take turns guessing if each object will float or sink.

Flashlight Reading

Grab a torch and a few of your favourite books, turn off the lights and jump under the covers. Things are so much more fun in your own little hidey hole especially when you can make it glow with light. You could even try making up your own stories in your secret bed cave!

Tongs Transfer

All you need are two bowls, a pair of tongs and a selection of items to transfer from one bowl to the other. Try objects of different shapes — round, square, long and thin, as well as different textures — a rock and a cotton ball for example. Encourage your child to practise their counting as they go.

Window Drawing

Find a comfortable place to sit with your child near a door or window
and encourage them to draw what they see outside. Maybe there are big
thunderclouds, muddy puddles or scattered leaves. Are there any birds
in the trees or insects scuttling past? Can you see the neighbours' dog?
Perhaps there is even a rainbow!

Make A Bag For Charity

The idea of helping others is a wonderful value to instill in your children.
Grab a bag and go through their drawers and cupboards with them to find things
for charity — look for toys, books and clothes they no longer need.

Write A Letter To A Loved One

There is nothing nicer than getting a hand written note in the mail. Why not surprise a loved one and help your child pen a letter to an aunt, uncle, friend or grandparent. Perhaps they could tell them what they love about them, or what they did today. You could even include a drawing to brighten their day.

DON'T FORGET TO ...

 Make pancakes for dinner

 Ask them what their favourite part of the day was

 Dance in the rain

 Follow a rainbow

Conclusion

If all else fails, don't worry — being bored is good for kids. Sometimes the best way to entertain your child is to not entertain them at all. When children run out of things to do they are forced to use their imagination.

Pretend play in a child's early years lays a strong foundation for physical, social and emotional wellbeing that lasts a lifetime. A child's imagination is a wonderful gift that won't last forever, so make the most of this precious age.

Thank you

An enormous thank you to: Jan Filipovic, Kristian Watts, Allen Elliott, Krissie Rogers, Amber Toms, Kirsten McKerrell, Doug Elliott, Shelley Lawnikanis, Stephanie Tait and Jasmine Standfield.

Stay in Touch

 Visit our website
www.busylittlekids.com.au

 Follow us on Instagram

 Like us on Facebook

 Busy Little Kids for iPhone

 Busy Little Kids for Android